12 THINGS
YOU (PROBABLY) DIDN'T
KNOW
ABOUT
EASTER

Also by Bob Lepine:

The Four Emotions of Christmas

12 THINGS
YOU (PROBABLY) DIDN'T
KNOW
ABOUT
EASTER

BOB
LEPINE

10 Publishing
a division of 10 ofthose.com

British Library Cataloguing in Publication Data
A record for this book is available from the British Library

ISBN: 978-1-915705-56-3

Designed and typeset by Pete Barnsley (CreativeHoot.com)

Printed in Denmark

10Publishing, a division of 10ofthose.com
Unit C, Tomlinson Road, Leyland, PR25 2DY, England

Email: info@10ofthose.com
Website: www.10ofthose.com

1 3 5 7 10 8 6 4 2

CONTENTS

IT'S NO CHRISTMAS

Does Easter sneak up on you every year?

About the time you start to see buds on trees and set your clock ahead an hour, you suddenly find yourself thinking "When's Easter this year?" It's confusing because the date hops like a bunny from one year to the next. Christmas is so much easier!

Not only is the date of Christmas easier to remember, but unless you sequester yourself in some off-the-grid cabin in the woods, there's no way you can ignore Christmas. There are thousands of merchants who will make sure you don't forget that Christmas is coming. They're counting on you to make Christmas a big deal every year.

Easter? Well, chocolate and candy sales might go up a bit but, thankfully, you're unlikely to find yourself too out of pocket – or enjoying time off work. There was a time when what we now call Spring Break was officially the Easter holiday from school. The week off from school was always synched with Easter.

That was a generation ago. Today, the school holiday is scheduled for a random week in March or April. Any connection it might have with Easter is purely coincidental. Children may wake up to find a basket with candy waiting for them. A few local restaurants may offer a big buffet or a special menu. But for most people, Easter passes like a light spring breeze. Unnoticed.

Because families often travel together during the spring break from school, the hotel chain Travelodge in 2014 decided to see what British children – who do get time off at Easter – knew about the holiday. You know where this is going, right? It turns out that nearly half of the children in Britain had no idea that Easter was a religious holiday. A third of them said that Easter celebrates the birth of the Easter Bunny. Another 25% thought Easter is somehow connected to the invention of the chocolate egg. As for going to church on Easter, 37% of parents in the UK said they would be taking a holiday at the beach instead of taking children to an Easter service at church.

If Christmas is MVP of holidays, Easter is the overlooked bench player. Of course, the irony is that without Easter, there would be no Christmas. The two holidays are joined at the hip. They are the pillars of Christianity. Christmas is about the birth of Jesus Christ. Easter is about his death and the subsequent reports of a resurrection after his body had been interred in a crypt in Jerusalem.

If Jesus' life had ended with his arrest and execution, virtually no one today would know anything about him. We'd know nothing about his birth and no details of his life. He would be a footnote in the history of the Jewish people – a Rabbi who preached about love and forgiveness and reportedly performed miracles while attracting a small band of followers. Then died. End of story.

But when the news started to spread that this Rabbi had died and then somehow had come back to life again, people took note. The reports of this miracle spread throughout the Roman Empire. And because the news was received and believed by many, we have a holiday that still shows up on our calendar every spring all these centuries later.

Easter may not capture the attention of the culture the way Christmas does, but you have to admit the holiday has demonstrated staying power.

And yet, like the British school children who took the Travelodge survey, there are a lot of us who don't know much about Easter. Fear not! By the end of this little book, you'll have twelve facts under your belt ready for any Travelodge survey that comes your way.

THE EASTER BUNNY WAS A LITTLE LATE TO THE PARTY

German Lutherans were apparently the first to imagine a giant Easter Bunny back in the 17th century – a tall rabbit carrying his Easter basket and dispensing eggs and candy to good girls and boys. He was kind of springtime Santa Claus with floppy ears and a cotton tail. In German folklore, it's the Easter Bunny who hides the eggs and delivers the Easter baskets on Easter eve.

It wasn't until the 20th century that the Easter Bunny was given a proper name. After cowboy singer Gene Autry scored a hit with "Rudolph the Red Nosed Reindeer" and "Here Comes

Santa Claus," he turned his attention to Easter. He recorded "Here Comes Peter Cottontail" in 1950, and it peaked at number 3 on the country songs chart, further establishing the Easter Bunny's reputation as central to the holiday.

But of course, Easter didn't originate with the Easter Bunny. To really score points on an Easter knowledge test you have to dive all the way back to the 1st century AD and to Roman-occupied Jerusalem. The Jewish people flocked to the capital each year to celebrate Passover, the festival remembering their escape from enslavement in Egypt many centuries earlier.

One particular year, sometime between AD 30 and AD 33, Jerusalem was in a frenzy. A popular local preacher and miracle worker had entered the capital a few days earlier to cheering crowds, but tension ran deep. The religious leaders had long hated Jesus of Nazareth and suddenly everything came to a head as one of Jesus' closest friends offered to sell him out. Within days the crowds were shouting "Crucify!" Jesus was put to death on the day we now call Good Friday.

While the exact year of his crucifixion isn't settled, the timing of the event is documented. On the first day of the Passover celebration in Jerusalem, Jesus was nailed to a Roman cross and executed for sedition. And according to the biblical record, on the following Sunday, the tomb where Jesus' body had been laid after his execution was found to be empty. For hundreds of years before anyone had thought to dress up as a bunny, Christians were celebrating Jesus Christ's return to life following a brutal death. That's Easter in a nutshell.

For those who saw and spoke to and touched and ate meals with the risen Jesus, the resurrection was the confirmation that Jesus was not just a good moral teacher or even a miracle worker. The resurrection of Jesus convinced them that their friend was both Savior and Lord, and they worshiped him as Christians have been doing ever since.

The death of Jesus occurred during the Jewish Feast of the Passover, a festival remembering the time when God set his people free from slavery in Egypt. To avoid the punishment of God back in Egypt, a lamb was sacrificed. Immediately links were drawn between the Passover and Jesus' death. Jesus himself told his followers that rather than a lamb being sacrificed for them, he would be sacrificed on the cross. To save people, Jesus died – keep reading for more on that!

Early Christians wanted to draw the connection between the ancient Jewish Feast of the Passover and the death and resurrection of Jesus. They called this new annual resurrection celebration the Pascha, or the Christian Passover. And 2,000 years later we have Easter, complete with the Easter Bunny and Creme Eggs (read on to see how on earth they fit in!), but Jesus still remains central to it all.

IT TOOK AN EMPEROR TO PIN DOWN THE DATE

The origins of Easter go back to the 4th decade of the 1st century, but when does the actual celebration of Easter date from? The short answer is AD 325. But there's much more to the story than that, of course.

The significance of Jesus' death and resurrection was recognized straight away by his first followers. In fact, for them, the celebration of Jesus' resurrection became an immediate weekly event. All of these men and women were Jewish and had spent their whole lives going to the local synagogues every

Saturday – the Sabbath – as prescribed in the Ten Commandments. But now they began meeting together on the first day of the week – our Sunday – as that's the day they believed Jesus had risen. Easter Sunday, every week!

But as with all holidays, it took a long time before an annual commemoration of the resurrection became widely recognized and officially sanctioned. Did you know for example, that it took over a century for the 4th of July to become an official holiday following the signing of the Declaration of Independence? Easter sits in good company.

So how is it that in AD 325, Easter became an officially established annual holiday throughout the Roman Empire? The answer to that question, as we're about to see, is connected to the reason why the date for Easter is not a fixed date on our calendars like Christmas is.

If you are someone who can't wait for Easter to come each year, you should know that the earliest possible date for Easter is March 22. You should also know Easter will not fall on March 22 in your lifetime. The last time Easter was celebrated on March 22 was in 1818.

The next time it will be celebrated that early will be in 2285.

The latest possible date for Easter is April 25. That was the date for Easter back in 1943. And you can mark your calendars now for the next time Easter will fall on April 25. It will happen again in 2038. Things get even more complicated when you start looking into which calendar you're working with – the Gregorian, the Julian, the Jewish… but that's another Google search.

The annual celebration of Easter, originally called Pascha, is connected to the Jewish Passover festival as Jesus was arrested and killed during Passover. While the connection between Easter and the Passover was clear to the early Christians, what wasn't clear was whether Easter should be on a fixed date or always on a Sunday. One group of early Christians held their feast on the 3rd day of Passover, whatever day of the week that happened to be. Others had their Pascha event on the Sunday of Passover, keeping with their practice of meeting and celebrating the resurrection on the first day of every week.

In AD 250, if you asked what day the Christian Pascha (our Easter) would be celebrated, the answer would have been "it depends which Christian group you're connected to." Not so helpful.

The issue was finally resolved in AD 325. The Roman Emperor Constantine had become a Christian, and he invited an incredible 1,800 Christian bishops to the first ever general council of the church. Only around 300 showed up to decide, amongst other more serious things, that Easter would happen on a Sunday – the first Sunday following the first full moon after the Spring Equinox. With that decided, Constantine made Pascha an official holiday throughout the Roman Empire. Sorted.

THE PAGAN GODDESS EOSTRE MAKES A BRIEF APPEARANCE

Interesting name for a holiday, right? We call Christmas "Christmas" because it's the Christ-Mass. We call Thanksgiving "Thanksgiving" because… You get the idea.

But Easter?

In many countries, it's more straightforward because the holiday goes by names tied more directly to the Jewish Passover. The first name for Easter was Pascha. In Greece, that's still what it's known as. Simple! Italians call it Pasqua.

In France, it's Pâques. In other European countries, the holiday goes by different names. In Poland, it's called Wielka Niedziela, "The Great Sunday." Finnish people call it Pääsiäinen which means "liberation." Hungarians, who give up meat in the weeks leading up to Easter, call their holiday Húsvét which literally means "to take meat."

But what about the English name for the holiday "Easter"? Here's where things get a bit uncertain. There's a sketchy backstory that may (or may not!) be connected to the name – it involves a pagan fertility goddess and an 8th-century Anglo Saxon monk named Bede the Venerable.

As a boy, Bede was sent by his parents to the Monkwearmouth Monastery in North East England. He became a well-regarded scholar and writer in his day. His best-known work is called *The Ecclesiastical History of the English People*, which gained him the title of "The Father of English History."

According to Bede, among the pagan gods and goddesses worshiped by the Anglo Saxons in the early Middle Ages, there was a goddess named Eostre who was said to rule the dawn. Every spring as the snows melted, the grass sprouted and the trees began to bud again, the people celebrated the rebirth of nature and the end of winter with a festival honoring Eostre.

As Christian missionaries came to Britain, they saw an opportunity. The people already had a springtime holiday that combined pagan spirituality with a festival. Why not co-opt the existing festival and repurpose it? Instead of celebrating warmer weather and longer periods of daylight, the missionaries turned the focus of the holiday to the story of the resurrection of Jesus. It just made sense. After all, the coming of spring every year serves as a powerful metaphor for God bringing new life to the world through the resurrection of Jesus.

The new converts to Christianity in the Anglo-Saxon world were happy to repurpose their annual spring festival with a higher and more noble focus. But old habits die hard. Even though the pagan goddess of the dawn was no longer the focus of the festival, they continued to use her name as the title of their celebration. Like I said, it's a little sketchy. Kind of like naming your first-born daughter after your old girlfriend.

That's one idea about where the word Easter came from. It's equally possible, and some believe more likely, that the name comes from a Latin phrase meaning "dawn" which became eostarum in Old High German and led to our word Easter.

Today, there are some Christians who err on the side of caution. They refuse to participate in any special Easter activities due to the potential links with pagan fertility rites. Others will commemorate Resurrection Sunday but won't use the word Easter for their celebration.

But most people today – current readers excepted! – have never even heard of the pagan goddess Eostre, so are unconcerned about the ex-girlfriend. Those who recognize the historical and spiritual nature of Easter now clearly see it for what it really is – a celebration of the resurrection of Jesus.

EGGS REALLY DO HAVE SIGNIFICANCE, CANDY NOT SO MUCH

Most years since 1878, on the Monday following Easter, the president of the United States has welcomed thousands of children onto the south lawn of the White House for an Easter egg roll, where they race to see who can most quickly push a brightly colored hard-boiled egg down a sloping hill. Since 1969, the US president has been flanked by a six-foot-tall costumed rabbit.

The annual White House Easter Egg Roll is not a one-of-a-kind event. There are well-established egg races that take place around Easter in Germany, Denmark, Lithuania and other countries throughout Europe. The idea of rolling an egg seems to be connected to Jesus' resurrection. Granted, the link isn't immediately obvious... but when Jesus was buried, he was laid in a tomb cut from rock and a huge stone was rolled over the entranceway to stop anyone getting in and stealing the body. On Easter Sunday morning, women went to the tomb wanting to put spices on Jesus' body as was their custom, but they didn't know how they were possibly going to move the stone. On arrival they found they needn't have worried as, to their astonishment, the stone had already been rolled away. Hence the egg rolling!

In the same way, Easter egg hunts have a connection to the resurrection of Jesus. The practice of hiding Easter eggs for children to find goes back as far as the time of the Protestant Reformer Martin Luther. In his day, eggs were hidden and hunted so children could get an idea of the joy and excitement the early disciples experienced when they heard the news that Jesus had risen from the grave.

Go even further back to the Middle Ages and people were dyeing eggs on the lead up to Easter. Red eggs symbolize Jesus' blood being shed on the cross, blue eggs symbolize God's love for his people and yellow eggs represent the sunlight that lit the empty tomb on the first Easter morning.

Colored hard-boiled eggs also appear to be connected to the Lenten fast that precedes Easter. Some Christians, through the years, have gone without certain foods in the weeks leading up to Easter. Eggs, dairy and meat were often on the verboten list during the Middle Ages. So when Easter arrived, people were delighted to find colorfully dyed hard-boiled eggs on the Easter table available to them for the first time in weeks.

These days, you'll need more than a hard-boiled egg to get anyone excited about Easter morning. Easter is the undisputed heavyweight champion for holiday candy consumption. And for that, in part, we have the son of a copper miner from Tywardreath in Cornwall, England, to thank.

Roscoe E. Rodda was born in the US in the 1860s. His parents emigrated from England and settled in Michigan, near Lake Superior. Roscoe learned the candy business as a young man working for the Gray, Toynton and Fox Candy Company in Detroit in the early 1880s. From there, he opened his own confectionary business in Cincinnati before eventually moving his wife and five children to Lancaster, Pennsylvania, where he founded the Rodda Candy Company in 1908 and began mass producing candy for nationwide sales.

Roscoe was trying to establish his business in the shadow of the newest, biggest candy mogul in America, Milton Hershey. He quickly realized that trying to compete head on with Hershey would never work. But in the early 1920s, he came up with an idea that would eventually carve out a profitable niche for him.

The candymaker observed the local German immigrants in Lancaster, Pennsylvania, who every year at Easter exchanged baskets full of eggs and non-edible figurines of rabbits. *What if,* he thought, *instead of eggs and carved objects, those baskets were full of candy?* Now there's an idea!

Roscoe launched a line of Easter-themed chocolate candy. He had solid chocolate bunnies, eggs, crosses, even a chocolate elephant. He also experimented with a labor-intensive custom-made marshmallow candy in the shape of baby chicks that he marketed under a variety of names, including "Rodda Marshmallow Peeps." Today, more than 2 billion marshmallow Peeps are sold each year, mostly at Easter.

Years before Roscoe Rodda began making Easter-themed candy in the US in the mid-1920s, two competing candy makers in England had been experimenting with making chocolate Easter eggs. The J.S. Fry and Sons company followed the custom work of chocolatiers from France and Germany and turned out its own version of a chocolate Easter egg in 1873. Two years later Richard and George Cadbury began manufacturing a variety of solid chocolate Easter eggs made from a pure cocoa butter that could be molded and smoothed.

The competitors merged in 1919, forming the British Cocoa and Chocolate Company. They continued operating as separate brands. Four years later, the new company began manufacturing fondant-filled eggs. But it took another 40 years, until 1971, before the now iconic Cadbury Creme Egg hit store shelves.

Today, the Cadbury company manufactures an impressive 500 million Creme Eggs each year. That number doesn't include the Cadbury Creme Eggs manufactured and sold in the US by... you guessed it, the Milton Hershey Company.

As it turns out, the connection between Easter and candy is more about capitalism at work than it is about a connection to the first Easter. Candy makers saw an opportunity for increased sales with Easter-themed candies. Consumers voted with their wallets.

MAKING HOT CROSS BUNS WAS ONCE A CRIMINAL OFFENCE

It's a pretty standard list of ingredients for a baker: milk, flour, yeast, butter and eggs, mixed together with sugar and the right spices, with some dried fruit thrown in. But in the right proportions, and in the right hands, that ingredient list can yield the mighty hot cross bun.

The hot cross bun originates from a still closely guarded secret recipe which can be traced back to St Albans Abbey in Hertfordshire, England. From 1361, Brother Thomas Rocliffe mixed together his own concoction of flour, eggs, fresh yeast, currants and grains of paradise or cardamom to make what became known as the Alban Bun. Brother Thomas marked his buns with a cross on the top of the unbaked dough, and the buns were distributed to feed the poor on Good Friday. The baking of the Alban Bun became an annual tradition at the monastery, where the buns continue to be baked and sold every spring. You can still buy an Alban Bun if you visit St Albans Abbey today.

During the late Middle Ages, the Alban Bun's popularity spread throughout the UK and beyond. The treats began to develop legendary status, with people believing they could cure diseases or bring good luck. It was thought the buns sold on Good Friday would never go stale. Hanging buns from the rafters of your home was said to be a way to ward off evil spirits. Sharing buns with someone special would supposedly guarantee a healthy friendship for the coming year.

As these superstitions grew, Queen Elizabeth I decided enough was enough. She passed a law limiting the sale of the Alban Bun. They could only be sold at Christmas, on Good Friday or for funerals.

But people, ever partial to the soft, spiced dough, got around the new regulations by experimenting with their own recipes and renaming the results as hot cross buns. When the monarchy realized there was no way to enforce a ban on the buns, the law was eventually rescinded.

But even the anti-Alban Bun Elizabeth I allowed the buns on Good Friday seeing the symbolic significance of the cross, which reminded the baker and consumer alike of the method by which Jesus was executed. Following the standard practice for condemned criminals, Jesus was nailed to a cross by Roman soldiers. Baking the buns on Good Friday fills a home with aromatic spices, bringing to mind the spices used to embalm the body of Jesus to prepare him for his burial. And as with all baked goods that incorporate yeast, the dough rises as part of the baking process, reminding people that Jesus rose from death to life.

If the association with crucifixion doesn't put you off, they're pretty fun to make and recipes can be found easily online. And if you're not baking on Good Friday, you can have the added thrill of breaking Queen Elizabeth I's anti-bun law. This only scratches the surface of lawbreaking associated with Easter. Things are about to get a lot more serious…

6

AT LEAST 18 LAWS WERE BROKEN TO CONDEMN JESUS TO DEATH ON GOOD FRIDAY

Ask an attorney to review the facts surrounding the arrest and conviction of Jesus and you'll get a unanimous verdict. No matter how you slice it, what happened to Jesus was a politically motivated miscarriage of justice that resulted in the wrongful murder of an innocent man.

For 3 years Jesus had traveled around and publicly taught vast crowds who flocked to hear him. The religious leaders in Israel didn't like Jesus or his followers one bit. His message was catching on, and his popularity was a threat to their power. They wanted him stopped. When Jesus started claiming he was equal with God, saying incredible things like "I and the Father are one,"[1] they suddenly had a way to deal with their "Jesus problem." Claiming to be equal with God was blasphemy, and under Jewish law blasphemy was a capital offense. The Jewish leaders agreed that Jesus had to be arrested and executed for his crime.

Finally, as the Jewish people were arriving in Jerusalem to celebrate the annual springtime Feast of the Passover, the leaders had their opportunity. One of Jesus' followers, Judas, came to them and, in exchange for money, offered to lead them to Jesus. They would make their move at night when there would be no crowds around him and he couldn't escape. Judas took soldiers to a grove of olive trees where he knew Jesus would be. Jesus was arrested and immediately taken for questioning despite it already being past midnight. For the next four hours, under the cover of darkness, Jesus was interrogated and declared worthy of execution by the religious authorities in their kangaroo court.

No less than 18 Jewish laws, designed to protect the accused, were violated. To begin with, those who sat as judge and jury were the very ones who'd bribed Judas to betray Jesus in the first place. It was a set up from the beginning. Jesus should have been tried in daylight hours. He wasn't. Capital offences couldn't be tried on the day before a holy day. Passover began the next evening. Trials had to last more than a day to allow time for consideration. No.

Those testifying against the accused had to be examined separately and their testimony had to agree. In Jesus' case multiple witnesses were bribed and they still couldn't agree. Those hearing the case should attempt to poke holes in the witnesses' stories in order to protect the accused man from false charges against him. Instead those hearing the case against Jesus had orchestrated the whole thing. The verdict could not be unanimous as this indicated a mob-like mentality among the tribunal. It was.

According to Jewish oral tradition, if the Sanhedrin condemned a man to death as often as once every 7 years, it was considered reckless. They were said to be running a slaughterhouse.[2]

But anyone reading the account of Jesus' trial, in his day or our day, would see immediately that it was a complete miscarriage of justice, designed to accomplish what the religious leaders had already determined they wanted to happen. They wanted Jesus done away with.

The council voted declaring Jesus worthy of death. He was beaten and spat upon by the temple guards. But there was an issue. Under Roman rule, the religious authorities had no power to put anyone to death. Enter Pontius Pilate...

7

THE ROMANS DIDN'T REALLY WANT TO KILL JESUS

The Roman officials and soldiers don't emerge well out of the Easter account. They certainly have innocent blood on their hands for Jesus' death, but they weren't as up for killing Jesus as we might expect.

In the 1st century AD, the nation of Israel was under Roman control. Rome ruled with a light touch. The emperor cared about collecting taxes and keeping the peace. The Jewish people were allowed to continue to practice their religious rituals and follow local laws and customs as long as they paid their taxes and didn't make trouble.

When Jesus began drawing crowds, telling people that the Kingdom of God was at hand, the Roman governor in Judea, Pontius Pilate, wasn't particularly worried. None of Jesus' followers were inciting violence or stirring up trouble. But the religious leaders now were.

It was about 4 a.m. on Good Friday. The religious leaders had condemned Jesus to death on the charge of blasphemy, but they had a problem on their hands. Their Roman overlords would not let them execute anyone. And the Romans would never execute someone on charges of blasphemy. Blasphemy against the God of Israel was not a crime against Rome.

So the Jewish leaders instituted phase two of their plan. As the sun rose, they went to Pontius Pilate and sought to persuade him that Jesus was a threat to Rome. Jesus regularly talked to crowds about the Kingdom of God being "his kingdom." They portrayed him to Pilate as a seditionist.

The religious leaders demanded Pilate have Jesus executed. Pilate did his own interrogation of Jesus, asking him about his kingdom. "My kingdom is not of this world," Jesus told him.[3]

Pilate came away convinced Jesus was not a threat to Rome. He told the Jewish leaders, "I find no guilt in him."[4]

Pilate looked for some way he could compromise with the Jewish leaders and satisfy their blood lust. He had Jesus flogged and beaten and brought him out before them, bloodied and bruised. "Does this man look like a dangerous rebel to you?" he asked them.

But they would not be deterred. They told Pilate that if he didn't execute Jesus, they would report him to the emperor as shirking his duties. "If you release this man, you are not Caesar's friend,"[5] shook Pilate. He was already on bad terms with his boss. At this point, he was afraid a negative report would put his job in jeopardy.

He caved. He handed Jesus over to his soldiers and ordered that he be crucified.

The history of Easter is rooted in the account of an innocent man who was the victim of corrupt religious leaders and a spineless Roman governor. He wasn't put to death because of anything he had done. In fact, the only charge against Jesus that could be made to stick was that he had claimed that he was equal with

God. That's a claim Jesus never denied. And the leaders, religious or civil, never considered that his claim might actually be true.

GOOD FRIDAY WAS THE
WORST DAY IN ALL HISTORY

There are many contenders for the worst day in history. President Franklin Delano Roosevelt famously called December 7, 1941, the day Japanese forces bombed Pearl Harbor, "a day that will live in infamy."

Sixty years later, when terrorists attacked the World Trade Center towers in New York and the Pentagon in Washington, DC, President George W. Bush called it a day when "our nation saw evil, the very worst of human nature."

Yet Christians all around the world agree "Good" Friday was the darkest day in all of human history. On that day, the Son of God was nailed to a cross and died. A few weeks later, one of Jesus' followers would tell crowds in Jerusalem, "you killed the Author of life."[6] When the Creator God turned up, he was put to death. So why do we call such a dark day – the worst day in all of history – Good Friday?

The "good" in Good Friday carries the older sense of "pious" or "holy," rather than "great" but it's still strange. For Christians, nothing could be more horrendous than killing the one they worship. What's holy and good about that?

The Bible tells us that Good Friday is good because of what the death of Jesus accomplished. Far from being unexpected, Jesus had repeatedly told his followers that he would be killed in the capital city, Jerusalem. Yet, he deliberately traveled there, ready to be arrested and then executed. The events of Good Friday had always been Jesus' plan.

Christians believe that God is a God of both justice and love. Being loving, he cares deeply for all people while, being just, he must deal with sin – *all* our wrongdoing – rather than ignore it.

And there's a lot of wrong in the human heart. It was all on display that first Good Friday.

The religious leaders conspired to put Jesus to death as he was a threat to their way of life. He challenged their authority. Their power and influence were at stake. They were so committed to their way of life that they were ultimately willing to kill Jesus to get their own way.

Stirred up by their leaders, and almost certainly bribed by them, a crowd shouted "Crucify!" when asked by Pontius Pilate what should happen to Jesus. The Roman ruler was willing to endorse the murderous plan because of his indifference toward God, and the desire to keep his own political career afloat. Even Jesus' closest followers abandoned him and hid away, scared they would be next in line for the death penalty.

None of these reactions on this terrible day came as a surprise to Jesus. He had taught that all people struggle to do the right thing, and that all people naturally prefer their own way to his. Justice must be served. But in an incredible act of unselfish love, Jesus chose to take the consequences and punishment justice demands.

Each Passover, as a sign of goodwill, the Romans released one prisoner of the people's choosing. Pilate offered to release Jesus, but the people called for a murderer named Barabbas to be freed instead. As Jesus was crucified that first Good Friday, Barabbas walked free. The Son of God died instead of Barabbas. What would have been Barabbas' worst day became his best.

Soon, Jesus' followers were telling whoever would listen that everyone could benefit from Jesus' execution in the same way. The worst day in history can turn our lives around too. Jesus died to pay the penalty for people's sin, all their wrongdoing and rejection of God, meaning anyone can walk free if they accept this gift from him.

"God so loved the world," the Bible says, "that he gave his only Son, that whoever believes in him should not perish but have eternal life."[7] Turning to Jesus means a person will not face eternal death, but will instead have eternal life with him forever.

Ever since, Christians have been telling everyone just how good the worst day in history really was.

YOU CAN SURVIVE CRUCIFIXION, BUT JESUS DIDN'T

At the heart of the Easter holiday is a remarkable proposition. Christians say that a man who was charged with crimes he did not commit was put to death on a Roman cross. His body was taken from the cross, wrapped in graveclothes, embalmed with spices and laid in a nearby tomb. A stone was rolled in front of the tomb, covering the opening. Then, some 36 hours later, that dead man shed his graveclothes and walked out of the tomb. Alive.

It's easy to see why for many people, the story of Jesus' resurrection is too fantastic to be believed. The idea that a dead man can come back to life does not fall easily on our modern, scientific ears.

As a result, some have wondered if it might be possible that Jesus didn't really die. Perhaps, the speculation goes, he simply passed out on the cross. Went into a coma. Became unresponsive. Once he was taken from the cross, wrapped in cloths and placed in a cool, dark cave, some theorize, he was revived. His supposed resurrection was instead a resuscitation.

This hypothesis has been called "The Swoon Theory." It's been around since the early 19th century but rose to some level of prominence in 1965 when a British scholar named Hugh Schonfield published a book called *The Passover Plot*.

Incredibly, we do have a record of someone surviving crucifixion. The Jewish historian Flavius Josephus tells of a case where he appealed to the Roman Emperor Titus Vespasian asking for mercy on behalf of three men who had already been crucified but were still alive. Titus granted the appeal and the three men were taken down from the cross. Under the care of a physician, one of the three men survived.

That's not what happened with Jesus. A careful examination of the historical documents from the eyewitnesses lays out clear and compelling evidence that Jesus did not survive his crucifixion. The evidence that supports the reality of his death is hard to refute.

The men who wrote the historical accounts of Jesus' death were certainly convinced that he had actually died on the cross. They knew that before the first nail was hammered into Jesus' hands and feet, his body was already in a terribly weakened state.

First, he had been awake all night. Three times during the night, guards and soldiers had beaten him. The final beating was the most severe. His already damaged body was lashed to a pole with his back exposed. A Roman guard using a whip known as a flagellum pounded Jesus' back.

The flagellum had several long leather strips connected to the handle. Attached to the leather strips were pieces of rock or glass or bone fragments, designed to tear into the flesh of the person being beaten. It was the job of the soldier executing the scourging to continue to strike the victim until muscle and tissue and bone and even bodily organs were exposed. Between the beating and the blood loss, it was not out of the question that the one being tortured would die before his body was ever nailed to the cross.

Once the scourging was complete, the condemned man was made to carry his own crossbeam to the location of his crucifixion. The crossbeam might weigh as much as 100 pounds. Jesus, we're told, collapsed under the weight of the beam on his way to the place where he was crucified. Soldiers had to enlist a bystander to carry the crossbeam the rest of the way to the execution site.

It's clear Jesus' body had been brutalized before the first spike went through his wrist. The loss of blood would have left him dizzy and weak. In this condition, it's no surprise he didn't remain alive for long once the crucifixion had begun.

Although it was sometimes the case that a crucified man could hang on a cross for two or three days before he died, there were times when the Roman soldiers sped up the process by breaking the legs of the condemned. This made it impossible for the victim to lift himself up to gasp for breath.

According to the accounts of Jesus' death, the guards had been ordered to accelerate the dying process. But when they came to break Jesus' legs, these trained executioners found he was already dead. To make sure, they took a spear and thrust it into the left side of Jesus' torso, aiming to rupture his heart. The spear wound produced a flow of both blood and a clear fluid which was likely the result of a pericardial effusion. The guards were convinced their victim was dead.

Even under scrutiny, the evidence is solid. Jesus did not swoon on the cross, only to awaken in an empty tomb, wrapped in graveclothes and suffering from the horrific injuries, only to somehow free himself and escape. One man might have survived crucifixion, but Jesus didn't.

10

DEAD MEN DO WALK

On Easter Sunday Christians from around the world celebrate Jesus walking out of the tomb, alive. Utterly impossible? Many think so.

The legal affairs editor at the *Chicago Tribune* newspaper, Lee Strobel, was an avowed atheist. It wasn't simply that he didn't believe in the existence of God. He was, by his own admission, hostile toward all religion, particularly Christianity. What he knew of the accounts about the life of Jesus – specifically the claims related to miracles and the assertion that he had come back to life following his crucifixion – he saw as a mixture of myth, legend, make-believe and wishful thinking.

As a journalist, Lee Strobel had been trained to be skeptical and to stay focused on facts and evidence. That training, mixed together with his natural inclination toward cynicism, led him to dismiss religion altogether.

Until the unthinkable happened. In 1979, eight years after Creme Eggs first hit the stores, Lee's wife started to believe that the biblical accounts of Jesus' life were true – including the account of his resurrection – and became a Christian.

Lee was convinced his wife had been conned by some kind of cult. As he saw it, it was his job to rescue her from herself and from the Christians with whom she had started spending so much time. Because he was a newspaper reporter, he had access to scholars and experts on a variety of subjects, including history and archeology. So he set out to build a case that he could present to his wife to convince her that her beliefs were unfounded and irrational.

The problem was, all the evidence stacked up *for* rather than *against* it…

Lee Strobel's story, told in his book *The Case for Christ*, is one of many accounts of skeptics from throughout history who put the claims of Christianity to the test only to come away convinced that Christianity is true and that what the Bible reports about the life, death and resurrection of Jesus holds up to careful scrutiny.

Here's a selection of what we know:

The tomb was empty. In spite of being heavily guarded by Roman soldiers, by the time the sun rose on the first day of the week, the grave where Jesus' body had been laid was empty. The guards had left their post (under penalty of death), apparently frightened away by someone or something. When the followers of Jesus arrived at the tomb to anoint the body of Jesus with spices, they were stunned to find the body was missing.

The body of Jesus was never located. When the reports began to circulate that Jesus had come back to life, both the religious and the civic leaders were desperate to stop the rumors. All they needed to do to put an end to the growing speculation was to produce the body of Jesus. They couldn't.

The accounts of Jesus' resurrection claim to be eyewitness testimonies, and read that way. Myths and legends grow up over time, as some details get forgotten and other details become exaggerated until generations later it's hard to know anything much with certainty. They have a "once upon a time" feel about them. In contrast, the accounts of Jesus' life come direct from the people who were there and contain many checkable details.

Hundreds of people claimed that they saw a resurrected Jesus. The Bible records a number of specific occasions where Jesus met with, spoke with and ate with his followers after his reported resurrection. Many of these men and women were at first naturally skeptical about what they were seeing. But over time, they became convinced that Jesus had come to life again. The early writings have a "go-and-ask-those-who-saw-Jesus-appear" quality to them. They're open to fact checking!

Tens of thousands of people who heard from the eyewitnesses were convinced. The number of Christians multiplied faster than rabbits! The spread of Christianity in the 1st century means that the message of the eyewitnesses to the resurrection was convincing. Certainly people throughout history have fallen under the spell of charismatic cult leaders who have convinced them to believe things that weren't true. But in the case of Christianity, there was no single charismatic leader leading people astray. Instead, there were dozens of men and women who had nothing to gain and who faced growing persecution who spread a consistent believable message about Jesus and his resurrection.

As fantastic as it may sound to modern ears, many have found the evidence for the resurrection of Jesus fits the data more convincingly than any other explanation. Certainly those who claim to have seen Jesus themselves were willing to die rather than deny it...

11

EASTER IS TO DIE FOR - LITERALLY

The first Christians recognized how central the resurrection of Jesus was to everything they believed about him. They didn't beat about the bush, as one early Christian wrote to other believers: "if Christ has not been raised, then your faith is useless… we are more to be pitied than anyone in the world."[8] The factual truth of Jesus' resurrection meant everything to them.

But not everyone at the time was quick to believe Jesus had come back to life that first Easter.

Jesus' half-brother, James, had never believed that his older sibling was who he claimed to be. He remained a skeptic throughout Jesus' life. There is no record of him having had anything to do with Jesus while he was alive. But James had a face-to-face encounter with Jesus after his resurrection. This long-standing skeptic became not only a believer, but a leader of the growing church in Jerusalem.

Maybe the best-known skeptic-turned-believer is Saul of Tarsus, whose story is found in the Bible book of Acts. He was a committed Jew and an early persecutor of Christians. Saul worked tirelessly to try to shut down the spread of the message of the resurrection. In his anti-Jesus zeal, he went from place to place overseeing the arrest of Christians, and when the very first Christian martyr was stoned to death in approximately AD 34, Saul approved heartily. But Saul's encounter with the resurrected Jesus turned him from a fervent persecutor of Christians to the premier missionary in the 1st century. Saul, also called Paul, traveled throughout Asia Minor, Greece and Italy to spread the word that Jesus was alive and to establish local churches in each of the cities he visited. Despite beatings and imprisonment, threats on his life and the prospect of execution, Saul stayed true to his conviction that Jesus rose from the dead and eventually was beheaded because of it.

He certainly wasn't the only one. History records that the men who were Jesus' closest disciples all spent the rest of their lives traveling throughout the Roman Empire telling others about the resurrection of Jesus. Before they saw him alive again, they were scared of the authorities and huddled in a locked room in case they were next in line for death. But something happened which transformed them. They claimed to see Jesus alive and realized that if Jesus had returned from the dead then all he had taught them was true. He really was and is God. Dying on the cross really did pay for all our sin and wrongdoing. He really is the only one who can conquer death. He really is to be trusted and followed. They went on to face incredible hardships and eventual martyrdom because of their testimony. Even in the face of death, not one of them ever recanted. Their belief that Jesus was resurrected was so rock solid, there was no way they could ever walk back on their claims of having seen him alive. The resurrection of Jesus cost them their lives.

JESUS WELCOMES DOUBTERS

For most people, Easter drifts gently by like a warm spring breeze. The Easter Bunny and egg hunts might make a brief appearance for the children and that's that.

But as we've seen, the bunnies and eggs and everything else that makes up the season is connected to something much bigger than the coming of spring. Easter points us to the most consequential event in all of human history. A man who claimed "I am the Son of God"[9] – and who backed up that claim with unprecedented wisdom and miraculous power, was put to death for crimes he did not commit, and then rose again to new life. To eternal life. To life beyond the grave.

Jesus met with his disciples the day he rose, but one of them had been missing. When the others told Thomas that Jesus was alive, he thought they were all crazy. His skepticism ran deep. "Unless I see in his hands the mark of the nails, and place my finger into the mark of the nails, and place my hand into his side, I will never believe."[10]

Thomas had witnessed all kinds of miracles when Jesus was alive. He had seen him turn water into wine. Heal a man who had been lame for decades. Heal another man who had been blind from birth. Thomas had been in the boat the night Jesus walked on the Sea of Galilee. And the time the wind and waves had become instantly calm after Jesus commanded a storm to stop. He had seen Jesus multiply loaves of bread and two fish so that thousands were fed. But when his friends told him Jesus had risen from the grave, it was all too much for him.

A week later, when Thomas was with the other disciples, still doubting the reports of a resurrection, Jesus suddenly appeared in the room with them. "Peace be with you," he said. And knowing what Thomas had said would be necessary for belief, Jesus told him, "Put your finger here, and see my hands; and put out your hand, and place it in my side. Do not disbelieve, but believe."[11]

When Thomas is talked about now, he's often referred to by the nickname that has become his trademark. He is known as "Doubting Thomas." But as the biblical account makes clear, Jesus was not put off by Thomas's skepticism.

Many months before, Jesus' disciples had been unable to help a boy tormented by demons. The boy's father came to Jesus and said to him, "If you can do anything, have compassion on us."

Jesus looked at the man and said, "'If you can'! All things are possible for one who believes."

The desperate father responded by saying, "I believe; help my unbelief!"[12]

And Jesus smiled and healed the man's son.

The father had doubts. He wanted to believe, but it was hard. That's where Thomas was. He wanted to believe that Jesus was alive, but it all just seemed impossible to him. If we're honest, we'd have to admit that Thomas's doubts are perfectly reasonable.

When Jesus showed Thomas his wounds, however, his doubts vanished, and it became crystal clear to him who Jesus was. He called him "My Lord and my God!"[13]

The message of Easter – and in fact, the message of the entire Bible – is a bold declaration that God himself came to live among us, as one of us. He lived a perfect life, in full obedience to his Father God. He then died a brutal death on a Roman cross, taking on himself the punishment we deserve for our sin – our wrongdoing and our rejection and indifference toward God. Three days later, his still heart began to beat, breath flowed into his lungs, eyes closed in death opened. He stood up from the slab of stone on which he had been laid and walked out of the grave, his body whole and strong. Jesus is alive and never to die again.

In the spring of 1929, C.S. Lewis found himself in a place he never expected to be. After wrestling with his own skepticism and doubts about the deity of Jesus and the reality of his resurrection, Lewis came to a point where, in his words, he finally "admitted that God was God, and knelt and prayed: perhaps, that night, the most dejected and reluctant convert in all of England." Lewis goes on to say, "I did not then see what is now the most shining and obvious thing; the Divine humility which will accept a convert even on such terms."[14]

If you find yourself like Doubting Thomas or C.S. Lewis, wrestling with doubt and thinking, "this can't possibly be true," Jesus invites you to bring your doubts to him. Take a first step of faith. Come to him saying, "Lord, I want to believe. Help my unbelief." If you're truly open to believing and following God, God will knock down the obstacles. He is gracious and kind to all who want to believe.

And there is good news for those who will eventually come to a place where, like Doubting Thomas, they can say with confidence that Jesus is "my Lord and my God." The message of Easter is that for all who believe, your sins have been forgiven. You have been redeemed. The barrier between you and God has been removed. He welcomes you into his family as his child.

Very good news indeed.

CONCLUSION

IT'S NO FUNERAL

You (probably) know a lot more about Easter now you've got to the end of this book. But, when digging into the events of the first Easter, it quickly becomes clear that there's more to all this than just general knowledge. According to Jesus himself, his death and resurrection have implications for every human being who has ever lived or will ever live. That includes you and me.

Once Jesus was challenged by a woman grieving for her brother. Martha couldn't understand why Lazarus had died. Jesus answered her with a profound claim:

I am the resurrection and the life. Whoever believes in me, though he die, yet shall he live, and everyone who lives and believes in me shall never die. Do you believe this?[15]

It's a question Jesus asks everyone: Do you believe this? Jesus offers every person life beyond the grave because he died and rose again and has the power to carry us through death and out the other side. We need to trust in him, asking him to forgive our sin and follow him throughout our lives.

If you want to accept this offer of eternal life, you can pray to Jesus using Martha's answer: "Yes, Lord; I believe that you are the Christ [King], the Son of God."[16] By making Jesus our Lord, we choose his ways rather than our own. By trusting in Jesus' death and resurrection to save us we can be confident of eternal life with him.

This Easter, why not read Jesus' life story firsthand in one of the four Gospels, Matthew,

Mark, Luke or John which open the New Testament in the Bible. Alternatively, you could quiz a Christian with your questions or you could head to a local church and continue to investigate this life – and death – changing man who died on a cross and then walked out of the tomb.

NOTES

1   John 10:30, see also John 5:18 and John 12:45.

2   Boice, J. M. *The Gospel of John: an expositional commentary*, (Baker Books, 2005), p. 1389.

3   John 18:36

4   John 18:38

5   John 19:12

6   Acts 3:15

7   John 3:16

8   1 Corinthians 15:17–19, NLT

9   John 10:36

10   John 20:25

11   John 20:27

12   Mark 9:20–24

13   John 20:28

14   Lewis, C.S. *Surprised by Joy* (Geoffrey Bles Ltd.,1955), p. 217.

15   John 11:25

16   John 11:27

10 Publishing

10Publishing is committed to publishing
quality Christian resources that are biblical,
accessible and point people to Jesus.

www.10ofthose.com is our online
retail partner selling thousands of
quality books at discounted prices.

For information contact: **info@10ofthose.com**
or check out our website: **www.10ofthose.com**